Future SmartMinds

www.futuresmartminds.com

Welcome to the **FutureSmartMinds** family!

Thank you for choosing "**Future AI Expert: A Journey into the Exciting World of Artificial Intelligence**" from our **STEM Explorers Series: Ignite the Future**. Your decision to bring this adventure into your home or classroom is the first step in joining a wonderful journey of discovery and innovation that spans the captivating world of STEM (Science, Technology, Engineering, and Mathematics).

We kindly invite you to share your thoughts about "**Future AI Expert**" on Amazon. Your feedback helps us continue to improve and inspire more young minds. Your honest review will guide others in making their choice and encourage them to join us in shaping the future of our future smart minds.

Scan to Rate Us on Amazon

Once again, thank you for being a part of our FutureSmartMinds community. We're excited to have you with us on this journey.

Warm regards,

The **FutureSmartMinds** Team

www.futuresmartminds.com

Email: FutureSmartMindsKids@gmail.com

  @futuresmartminds

  @futuresmartminds

@ futuresmartminds

Scan to visit our website

Content	Page
Exploring Artificial Intelligence	**4**

Content	Page

Exploring Artificial Intelligence

Welcome to the fascinating world of Artificial Intelligence (**AI**)! In this adventure, we'll embark on a journey to uncover the secrets behind AI, understanding what it is and why it's so important in today's world. **Artificial Intelligence** refers to the capability of machines to imitate intelligent human behavior.

Imagine computers that can learn, reason, and solve problems like you! AI enables machines to understand, analyze, and interpret information, making decisions based on patterns and experiences.

AI Exciting Journey Through Time!

The story of **AI** is as much about innovation as it is about human ingenuity. Although "**Artificial Intelligence**" may sound futuristic, its inception can be traced back to the mid-20th century. The seeds were sown by brilliant minds like Alan Turing, who envisioned machines capable of intelligent behavior. The Dartmouth Conference 1956 marked the formal birth of **AI** as a field of study, laying the groundwork for a technological revolution.

Since then, **AI** applications permeated various industries, from healthcare and finance to education and entertainment. Autonomous vehicles, voice-activated assistants, and recommendation systems showcased the transformative potential of AI in shaping our everyday experiences. Now, **AI** stands as a beacon of innovation, offering solutions to complex problems and unlocking new frontiers of possibility.

AI In Everyday Life!

Imagine a world where your favorite games, helpful robots, and talking gadgets are brought to life by **AI**. This is the secret behind toys becoming smarter, games turning more exciting, and gadgets becoming your trusty companions. Venture into the domain of healthcare, where **AI** transforms into a superhero doctor. It analyzes pictures of our insides, comprehends the complexities, and aids doctors in providing faster and more accurate treatments.

In the domain of education, AI becomes your personalized guide, crafting lessons tailored just for you—a magical tutor who understands your unique way of learning.

AI Shaping Our World!

Imagine having your own magical assistant, like Siri or Alexa, who listens to your questions and helps you unravel the world's mysteries. These **AI** friends make our days brighter, easier, and more fun! Have you ever felt like a game knew you so well it was practically reading your mind?

That's the enchantment of **AI**—creating games that feel like personalized adventures, learning and adapting to your every move. And what about chatting with a robot that seems to understand every word you say? **AI** is the wizard behind these friendly robots, turning your words into actions and making you feel like you have magical friends.

Hands-On Adventures into AI

Get ready for hands-on adventures that will bring **AI** concepts to life. Through exciting activities, experiments, and projects, we will not only understand the wonders of **AI** but also unleash our creativity and problem-solving skills. **AI** can even be artistic! We'll dive into projects where **AI** generates art and music, showcasing its creative side. Imagine collaborating with a machine to create something entirely new and unique.

Get ready to be a **problem-solving** wizard yourself! We'll engage in activities where **AI** helps us crack codes, solve puzzles, and unravel mysteries. It's like having a brilliant teammate with a knack for solving brain teasers.

The Magical World of Pattern Recognition

Picture this: you're handed a puzzle, and instead of solving it, you teach a machine to do it for you. That's the magic of **pattern recognition** in **AI.** By understanding patterns, you guide machines to recognize shapes, colors, and even your favorite toys. It's like having a magical assistant that knows your every preference!

The Machine Learning Magic

Have you ever dreamed of teaching a machine to learn from experiences, just like you do? In **machine learning**, you seek to create your own innovative machine. Like a magical creature teaching new tricks, you'll witness machines evolving and adapting through fun experiments. It's like having a pet robot that grows wiser with every interaction!

The AI Art Studio

What if you could use **AI** to create art that dazzles the senses? Welcome to the **AI Art Studio**, where you become the artist, and **AI** is your magical paintbrush. Through interactive experiments, you'll discover how **AI** can turn your doodles into masterpieces and bring your wildest artistic dreams to life. It's like having a personal art tutor that turns your imagination into reality!

Chatbot Charms

Have you ever wished you could talk to a machine, and it would understand you like a close friend? Enter the world of **chatbot** charms, where you learn to create your own conversational **AI**. Through engaging experiments, you'll uncover the secrets of making machines chat just like you do. It's like having a magical friend who listens, understands, and responds with the charm of a witty companion!

Unlocking the Secrets of AI

As you embark on these hands-on adventures into AI, the enchantment continues to unfold. Each activity is designed to spark your imagination, encourage curiosity, and unveil the secrets of the magical world of Artificial Intelligence. So, get ready to empower your creativity as you dive into these interactive experiments and become the masters of AI magic!

(1) Scratch Adventure: Become a Code Wizard!

Embark on a magical journey into the world of coding with Scratch! You'll become a Code Wizard, discovering how to make characters come to life and create your very own digital stories, games, and animations. It's like having a magic wand; instead, you'll use cool coding blocks! Scratch is not just a programming language but a canvas for creativity. Here, you'll learn to command your very own characters, known as sprites, and tell them what to do, just like a wizard with their spells!

Instructions

Step 1: Enter the World of Scratch

➢ Zoom over to the **Scratch** website: https://scratch.mit.edu/

Or Click the **QR Code** to take you to the Scratch website.

➢ Create an account by clicking **Join Scratch (it is totally free!)** so you can save your work.

➢ Click on "Create" to start a new project.

Step 2: Gaze upon the Stage

➢ This is the large area on the right side of the screen where your Scratch project comes to life.

➢ It's like a theater stage where your characters, called sprites, perform actions, tell stories, or play games.

➢ You can change the backdrop of the stage to different scenes or colors.

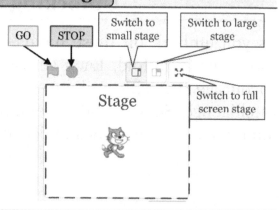

Step 3: Meet the Sprites

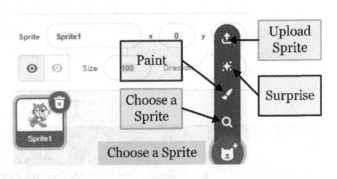

➢ The **Sprite list** is located beneath the **Stage Area**, this is where all your sprites (characters or objects) are listed.
➢ You can add new sprites from a library, draw your own, or upload images.
➢ Each sprite has its own scripts, costumes, and sounds.

Step 4: Explore the Block Palette

➢ This is the area on the left side, filled with colorful code blocks.
➢ These blocks are categorized into different functions such as **Motion, Looks, Sound, Events, Control, Sensing, Operators, and Variables**.
➢ You can drag these blocks and snap them together to create scripts.

Step 5: Check the Coding Area

➢ The large space in the center is where you build your scripts by snapping together the blocks from the Block Palette.
➢ Each sprite has its own coding area, so you can switch between sprites to see and edit their scripts. It's like a canvas where you paint with code blocks to bring your sprites to life.

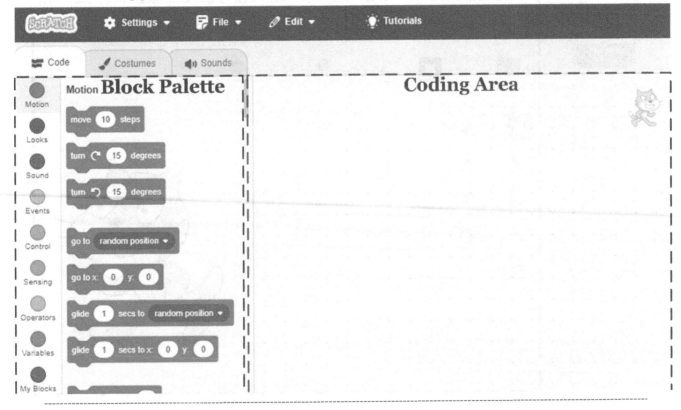

Step 6: Get Familiar with the Toolbar

➤ At the top of the screen, the toolbar has options to save your work, share your project, see in full screen, and more.

➤ You can also access the tutorial section here for helpful guides on using Scratch.

Toolbar

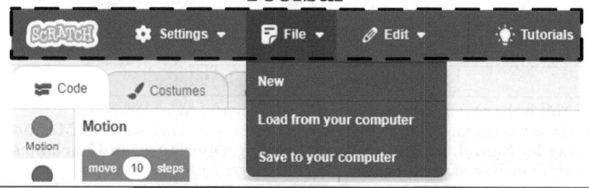

Step 7: Discover the Costumes Tab

➤ The Costumes tab lets you edit the appearance of your sprites.

➤ You can draw costumes, import images, or choose from the library.

➤ Each sprite can have multiple costumes for animation.

Costumes Tab

Step 8: Check the Sounds Tab

- ➢ Here, you can add sound effects and music to your sprites.
- ➢ You can record your own sounds, import, or choose from the Scratch library.

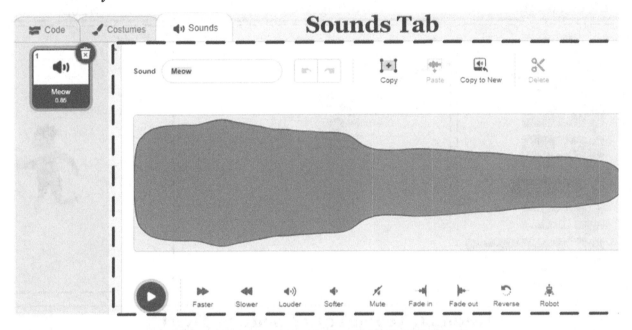

Step 9: Summon Your First Sprite

- ➢ Click on the magical 'Choose a Sprite' button.
- ➢ Pick a sprite to be your trusty sidekick.

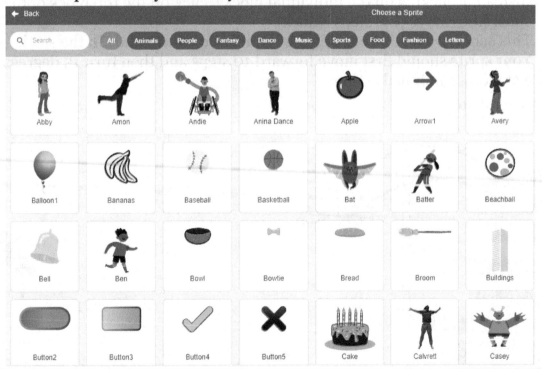

Step 10: Make Your Sprite Dance

➤ Dive into the '**Motion**' spells in your **Block Palette**.
➤ Drag the "**move (10) steps**" spell to your **Coding Area**.
➤ Click the spell and watch your sprite take its first steps!

Step 11: Teach Your Sprite to Twirl

➤ Seek out the "**turn ↻ 15 degrees**" spell.
➤ Drag the "**turn ↻ 15 degrees**" block and attach it directly underneath the "**move (10) steps**" block. They should snap together.
➤ Instead of clicking on the individual blocks, click on the top block of the stack (the "move (10) steps" block).
➤ This action will execute the entire sequence of commands in the stack.
➤ Your sprite should first move forward 10 steps and then turn 15 degrees in a smooth, combined action.

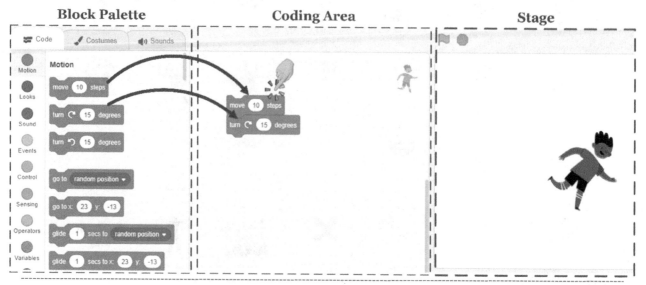

- ➢ Mix and match different '**Motion**' spells.
- ➢ Discover spells like "**go to random position**" to teleport your sprite.
- ➢ Build a tower of spells and see the magic unfold!

Step 13: Cast a Starting Spell

- ➢ Find the "**Events**" spellbook and choose "**when green flag clicked**".
- ➢ Stack your motion spells underneath it.
- ➢ Wave your cursor over the **green flag** and watch your code come to life!

Coding Area   **Stage**

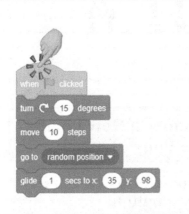

Step 14: Explore the Forest of Blocks

- ➢ Try spells from the '**Looks**', '**Sound**', and '**Control**' books.
- ➢ Each spell does something special – experiment to find your favorites!

Step 15: Save Your Magical Creation

- ➢ If you're a registered coding wizard, you can save your adventure by clicking 'File'> 'Save now.'

The Science Behind Scratch

Discovering the Magic of Coding:

Just like wizards use spells, in Scratch, you use colorful code blocks to make cool things happen. Every time you snap those blocks together, you're like a coding wizard casting a spell!

Science of Commands and Actions:

When you tell your sprite to move or turn, you learn about cause and effect – a basic science concept. It's like saying, "Hey, if I do this (click a block), then that happens (my sprite moves)."

(2) AI Chat Pal: Create Your Own Chatbot!

Imagine having a digital friend who can answer your questions and chat with you. That's exactly what we will build using Scratch – a fun, friendly chatbot! This isn't just cool; it's a step into the world of Artificial Intelligence (AI), where computers learn to understand and talk like humans. Let's get coding and bring our AI Chat Pal to life!

Chatbot

Instructions

(1) Set Up Your Scratch Project

» Open **Scratch** and start a new project.

» Delete the default cat sprite by right-clicking it and selecting 'delete'.

(2) Choose a New Sprite for Your Chatbot

» Click the '**Choose a Sprite**' button.

» Select a character you like to be your Chat Pal.

(3) Create the Chat Interface

» Go to the '**Backdrops**' and design a simple background for your chat interface.

» You can add colors, shapes, or any design that feels like a chat space.

(4) Start Coding Your Chat Pal

» Click on your sprite and go to the 'Events' block category.

» Drag "when this sprite clicked" block to the coding area.

(5) Add Interaction

» From 'Sensing', add "ask [What's your name?] and wait" block under the event block.

» This block will prompt the user to enter their name.

(6) Use the Answer Block

» The "answer" block (found under 'Sensing') holds the response entered by the user.

» It will automatically store the name entered after the "ask and wait" block.

(7) Create a Greeting

» Go to the 'Operators' and drag the "join [hello] [answer]" block.

» Ensure there's a space after "hello" within the brackets.

» This will combine the word "hello" with the user's name.

(8) Insert the Answer Block

» Drag the "answer" block from the 'Sensing' category.

» Place this block into the second space of the "join [hello] [ ]" block.

(9) Make the Chatbot Speak

» From 'Looks', grab a "say" block and connect it below your "ask" block.

Insert the "join [hello] [answer]" block inside the "say" block.

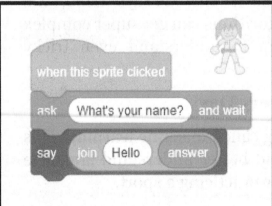

(10) Test Your AI Chat Pal

» Click the green flag.

» Click your sprite and type your name when prompted.

» Your chatbot should now respond with "Hello [Your Name]".

(11) Save Your Creation

» Name your project and save it for future tinkering.

The Science Behind AI Chat Pal

When you created your chatbot in Scratch, you took the first step into the world of **AI and programming**. This is just the beginning! As technology advances, who knows what cool chatbots you might create or interact with in the future!

Understanding Language: It's All About Patterns

AI chatbots are intelligent programs that can understand and respond to our words. But how? Well, it's all about recognizing patterns in language. Just like you learn to recognize words and sentences, chatbots use algorithms (problem-solving methods) to spot patterns in what we type or say.

Algorithms: The Brain of a Chatbot

Algorithms are sets of instructions that tell the chatbot what to do. In our Scratch project, we used simple algorithms, like if someone says "hello," the chatbot responds back with "hello!" These algorithms can get super complex in more advanced chatbots, allowing them to understand even tricky sentences!

Machine Learning: Getting Smarter Every Day

Some super advanced chatbots use something called machine learning. This means they can learn from conversations and better understand language over time, just like you learn from studying or practicing a sport.

So, next time you chat with a bot, remember the cool science behind it. You're not just talking to a machine; you're interacting with a program that uses algorithms and machine learning to understand you. Keep exploring, and maybe one day, you'll create chatbots that amaze the world!

(3) Math Puzzle Solver: The AI Math Whiz!

Ready for a fun challenge? Let's build an AI Math Puzzle Solver in Scratch! Imagine a game where you're not alone in solving math puzzles; you have a smart AI buddy to help you. This is not just any game; it's your first step into the fascinating world of AI and mathematics. Let's dive in and create a game where solving math is more fun than ever!

Instructions

(1) Set Up Your Scratch Project

» Open **Scratch** and start a new project.

» Delete the default cat sprite by right-clicking it and selecting 'delete'.

(2) Choose a Sprite for Your AI Math Helper

» Click the '**Choose a Sprite**' button.

» Select a character you like to be your AI Math Helper.

(3) Design Your Game Background

» Click on '**Choose a Backdrop**'.

» Select or design a backdrop that looks like a classroom or a fun math-themed environment.

(4) Create a Math Puzzle Challenge

» Start by dragging the "**when green flag clicked**" block from the '**Events**' section into the Coding Area.

» Use the "**ask [What is 2 + 2?] and wait**" block from the '**Sensing**' category.

» This block will ask the player a math question.

(5) Create a Logic Check

» Drag an "**if then else**" block from the '**Control**' category into your script.

» Inside the "**if**" part, place an "**=**" block from the '**Operators**' category.

(6) Check the Answer

» In the first slot of the "**=**" block, place the "**answer**" block from the '**Sensing**' category.

» In the second slot, type the correct answer to your math question (e.g., 11 for "What is 9 + 2?").

(7) Correct Answer Response

» In the "**then**" part of the "**if then else**" block, add a "**say [Great job!] for 2 seconds**" block from the '**Looks**' category. This is for when the player's answer is correct.

(8) Incorrect Answer Response

» In the "**else**" part, add a "**say [Try again!] for 2 seconds**" block. This is for when the player's answer is incorrect.

(9) Test Your Game

» Click the green flag.

» Click on your sprite and answer the math question.

» The program should respond with **"Great job!"** if the answer is correct, or **"Try again!"** if it's incorrect.

(10) Add More Questions

» You can duplicate this script and modify it for different math questions, increasing the difficulty as you like.

The Science Behind the Math Puzzle Solver

Algorithms in Action

You've used basic algorithms to create this game. An algorithm is a set of instructions that help solve problems – like checking if a math answer is correct.

AI and Problem Solving

AI in real life often works like this. It can analyze problems (like math puzzles) and provide solutions based on its programming.

Learning Through Games

This game makes learning math fun and interactive. Educational games are a great way to combine learning with play, which is super effective for remembering what you learn.

Coding Skills for the Future

By creating this game, you're learning to think like a programmer. These skills are super important as technology becomes a bigger part of our lives.

Real-World Applications

AI is used in many educational apps and games to help students learn. Your Scratch project is a simple version of what developers do in the real world.

(4) Weather Wizard: AI Weather Prediction Tool Based on Patterns

Ready to predict the weather with your own AI tool? Let's embark on an exciting journey to create the "Weather Wizard" in Scratch! This isn't just about guessing if it's sunny or rainy; it's about understanding patterns and using AI to predict the weather. Get ready to mix coding with science and become a weather prediction expert!

Instructions

(1) Setting Up Your Scratch Project

» Open **Scratch** and start a new project.

» Delete the default cat sprite by right-clicking it and selecting 'delete'.

(2) Choose Your Weather Wizard Sprite

» Click the '**Choose a Sprite**' button.

» Select a character you like to be your Weather Wizard

(3) Creating a Weather Backdrop

» Select '**Choose a Backdrop**'.

» Pick or design a backdrop that represents different weather conditions (sunny, rainy, cloudy, etc.).

(4) Programming Weather Predictions

» Start by dragging the "**when green flag clicked**" block from the '**Events**' section into the Coding Area.

» Use the "**ask [What's the season?] and wait**" block from the '**Sensing**' category.

» This allows the player to input a season (like 'summer' or 'winter').

(5) Create Conditional Statements

» Drag an "**if then**" block from the '**Control**' category for each season you want to include (e.g., one for summer, another for winter).

» Inside each "**if then**" block, you'll check if the user's input matches a specific season.

(6) Adding Seasonal Weather Responses

» In the hexagonal slot of the "**if then**" block, place an "**=**" block from the '**Operators**' category.

» Drag the "**answer**" block from the '**Sensing**' category and snap it into the first slot of the "**=**" block.

» In the second slot of the "**=**" block, type the name of the season ("Summer", "Winter").

(7) Command Your Weather Wizard to Speak

» Inside the "**then**" part of each "**if then**" block, add a "say" block from the '**Looks**' category.

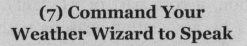

(8) Respond with Weather Predictions

» In the "**say**" block, type in the weather prediction that corresponds to the season you're checking.

» Example: If it's summer, the wizard might say, "It's likely to be sunny!"

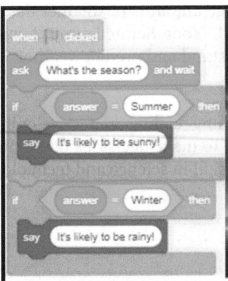

(7) Testing Your Weather Wizard

» Click the green flag.

» Interact with your Wizard by typing a season.

» See how it predicts the weather based on the season.

(8) Repeat and Save Your Work

» Create similar "**if then**" blocks for other seasons with appropriate weather predictions.

» Name your project '**Weather Wizard**' and save it.

The Science Behind the Weather Wizard

Pattern Recognition

This activity teaches basic pattern recognition, a core part of AI. You're teaching the computer to make predictions by associating seasons with typical weather patterns, much like how AI works in real-life applications.

Meteorology Basics

Understanding seasons and weather patterns is fundamental in meteorology (studying weather). This activity gives you a glimpse into how weather forecasts are made.

AI in Weather Forecasting

AI and complex algorithms analyze huge amounts of weather data to make accurate predictions in the real world. Your Scratch project is a simple version of how AI can be used to understand and predict weather.

Coding and Logical Thinking

By creating this AI tool, you're learning coding and developing logical thinking skills. You're figuring out how to make decisions based on data (in this case, seasons), which is a valuable skill in science and technology.

(5) Linguistic Quest: AI-Language Adventure

Linguistic Quest

Are you ready to embark on a thrilling quest around the world with AI? Introducing "AI Linguistic Quest," a fun and interactive game where you'll learn new words in different languages. With your AI guide, you'll hop from country to country, discovering how to say hello, thank you, and more in various languages. It's not just a game; it's a journey into the heart of cultures and the future of learning. Let's start this exciting adventure in Scratch and unlock the secrets of languages with the help of AI!

Instructions

(1) Launch Your Scratch Project

» Go to **Scratch** and start a new project.
» Delete the default sprite by right-clicking on it and selecting 'delete'.

(2) Choose a Sprite for Your AI Language Guide

» Click on '**Choose a Sprite**'.
» Pick a character that will be your AI language guide.

(3) Design Your Language Learning Environment

» Click on '**Choose a Backdrop**'.
» Select or create a backdrop that looks like a globe or a map to represent different countries.

(4) Program the Language Question

» Use "**when green flag clicked**" block from 'Events.'
» Use the "**ask [What language do you want to learn the words in? English of Spanish?] and wait**" block from the '**Sensing**' category.

(5) Set Up Conditional Statements

» Drag an "**if then else**" block from the '**Control**' category for the player's choice.

» Inside the condition, use an "**=**" block from the '**Operators**' category.

» Place the "**answer**" block in the first space of the "**=**" block and type "**English**" in the second space.

(6) English to Spanish Translation

» If the player chooses "English", you can then ask them which word they want to translate to Spanish.

» Use another "**ask [Which word do you want to translate to Spanish? (Hello, Thank you, Goodbye)] and wait**" block.

(7) Check the English Word

» Use multiple "**if then**" blocks to check for each English word.

» Inside each "**if then**" block, check if the player's answer matches an English word like "Hello", "Thank you", or "Goodbye".

(8) Respond with Spanish Translation

» In the "then" part, use a "**say [Hola] for 2 seconds**" block if the English word is "Hello".

» For "Thank you", use "**say [Gracias] for 2 seconds**".

» For "Goodbye", use "**say [Adiós] for 2 seconds**".

(9) Spanish to English Translation

» In the "**else**" part, handle the Spanish to English translation.

» If the player chooses "Spanish", you can then ask them which word they want to translate to English.

» Use another "**ask [Which word do you want to translate to English? (Hola, Gracias, Adiós)] and wait**" block.

(10) Respond with English Translation

» Use multiple "**if then**" blocks to check for each English word.

» In the "then" part, use a "**say [Hello] for 2 seconds**" block if the Spanish word is "Hola".

» For "Gracias", use "**say [Thank you] for 2 seconds**".

For "Adiós", use "**say [Goodbye] for 2 seconds**".

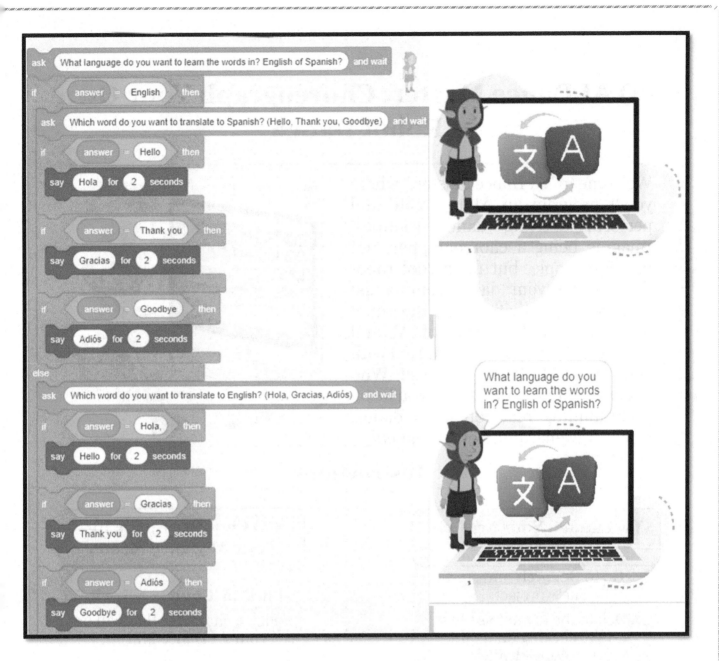

The Science Behind the Linguistic Quest

AI and Language Learning: AI systems can process and teach languages by recognizing patterns in words and sentences, much like how you're programming your Scratch game.

Global Connectivity: Knowing multiple languages is a superpower in our interconnected world! It helps in understanding different cultures and connecting with more people.

Technology in Education: This game mirrors how educational apps use technology to make learning fun and interactive. You're experiencing how games can be powerful tools in education.

(6) AI Dance Master: Choreograph Your Own Robot Dance

Welcome to "AI Dance Master," where you'll program an AI to create and perform dazzling dance routines. Imagine being a choreographer, not just for people, but for a cool robot that follows your dance commands! This exciting activity blends the fun of dancing with the magic of AI and coding. Let's get the party started with your own AI dance routines! Who knows, maybe one day, you'll be programming real robots to dance, work, or even explore other planets!

Instructions

(1) Launch Your Scratch Project

» Go to **Scratch** and start a new project.

» Delete the default sprite by right-clicking on it and selecting 'delete'.

(2) Choose a Sprite for Your AI Dance Master

» Click on '**Choose a Sprite**'.

» Pick a character that will be your AI Dance Master.

(3) Design a Dance Stage

» Click on '**Choose a Backdrop**'.

» Pick a backdrop that looks like a dance stage or a party setting.

(4) Capture the User's Command

» Use "**when green flag clicked**" block from '**Events.**'

» Use the "**ask [What dance move should I do? (spin, jump, slide)] and wait**" block from the '**Sensing**' category.

(5) Check the Dance Command

» For each dance move, drag an **"if then"** block from the **'Control'** category into your script.

» Inside the condition of the **"if then"** block (the hexagonal space), place an **"="** block from the **'Operators'** category.

» In the first slot of the **"="** block, place the **"answer"** block. In the second slot, type the name of the dance move ("spin", "jump", "slide").

(6) Program the Dance Actions

» In the **"then"** part of the **"if then"** block, add motion blocks from the **'Motion'** category to make the sprite perform the dance move.

» For example, if the command is "spin," you might use a **"turn ↻ 15 degrees"** block several times to make the sprite spin.

(7) Program the Jump Action

» For "jump," use **"change y by 10"** to make the sprite move up.

» Add a **"wait 0.5 seconds"** block from the **'Control'** category. This pause allows the jump to be visible.

» Add a **"change y by -10"** block to move the sprite back down.

(8) Program the Slide Action

» For "slide," use **"move 10 steps"** to slide in one direction.

» Add a **"wait 0.5 seconds"** block from the **'Control'** category. This pause allows the slide to be visible.

» Add a **"move -10 steps"** to slide back.

(9) Add Music

» You can also add a **"play sound"** block from the **'Sound'** category to play music while the sprite dances.

(10) Test and Save Your AI Dance Master Project

» Click the green flag.

» Enter a dance move and watch your AI perform it.

» Title your project 'AI Dance Master' and save it.

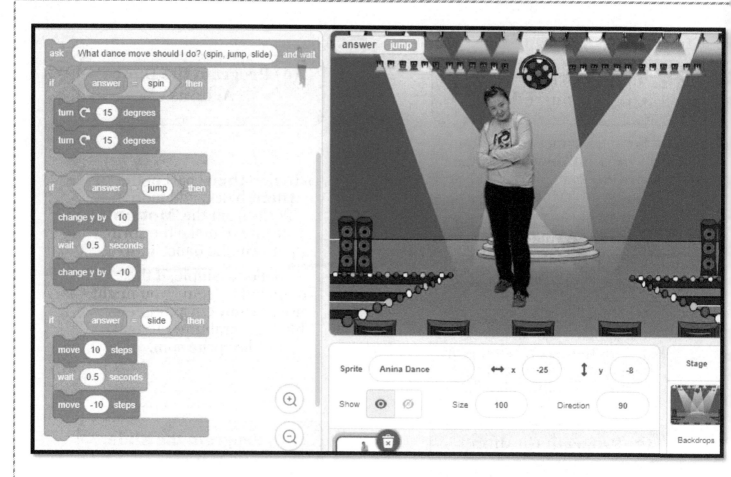

The Science Behind the AI Dance Master

Programming and Creativity

This activity combines coding with artistic expression. You're learning how algorithms can be used for calculations and creative purposes like dance.

Understanding AI and Motion

AI in robotics often involves programming movements. By creating dance routines, you see how roboticists program robots to move in specific ways.

The Power of Instructions

Each dance move you program teaches you to give clear instructions to computers. This skill is critical in programming, where precise commands lead to desired outcomes.

Real-World Applications

In the real world, choreographing robots is not just for fun. It's used in entertainment, manufacturing, and more. Robots that can move precisely are crucial in many industries.

(7) Symphony Wizard: AI Musical Maestro

Get ready to dive into the magical world of AI and music! In this exciting adventure, you'll become a musical maestro, teaching a smart computer how to compose its very own melodies. Imagine creating tunes that have never been heard before, all with the help of artificial intelligence. Let's embark on this melodic journey and make some musical fun!

Instructions

(1) Launch Your Scratch Project

» Go to **Scratch** and start a new project.

» Delete the default sprite by right-clicking on it and selecting 'delete'.

(2) Choose a Sprite for Your AI Symphony Wizard

» Click on '**Choose a Sprite**'.

» Pick a character that will be your AI Symphony Wizard.

(3) Upload Your Symphony Sound

» Go to the '**Sounds**' tab near the top of the screen.

» Click on the '**Choose a Sound**' icon (looks like a speaker) and select '**Upload Sound**'.

» Choose a symphony sound file from your computer. Ensure the file format is supported by Scratch (like .mp3 or .wav).

(4) Lay Down the First Note

» Start by dragging the "**when green flag clicked**" block from the '**Events**' section into the Coding Area. This will be the starting point of your program.

» Find a "**forever**" loop block in the '**Control**' section and snap it beneath the green flag block. This loop will keep your melody playing continuously.

(5) Create an AI-Inspired Composition

» Inside the forever loop, use the "**play sound [your uploaded symphony sound]**" block.

» After the sound block, add a "**wait 1 seconds**" block from the '**Control**' section. You can adjust the time to create a pause between repeats of your symphony sound, giving a remix effect.

(6) Experiment with Sound Effects

»Under the '**Sound**' category, locate the blocks for "**set pitch effect to [10]**" and "**set pan left/right effect to [10]**".

» The pitch effect changes the highness or lowness of a sound, and the pan effect moves the sound between the left and right speakers or headphones.

» Drag these blocks into your script to see how they change the symphony sound. Play around with the numbers to explore different levels of effect.

(7) Adjust the Volume

» Use "**change volume by [-10]**" or "**set volume to [volume]%**" to alter the loudness of your symphony sound.

» Experiment with placing these blocks at different points in your script to see how the volume changes affect the start, middle, or end of the symphony playback.

(8) Combine Effects and Save Your Project

» Try combining the pitch and pan effects with volume adjustments. For instance, you could start with a normal pitch, then gradually increase the pitch and decrease the volume to create a unique fading effect.

»Make sure to save your project after each significant change. This allows you to keep track of your experiments and share them with others.

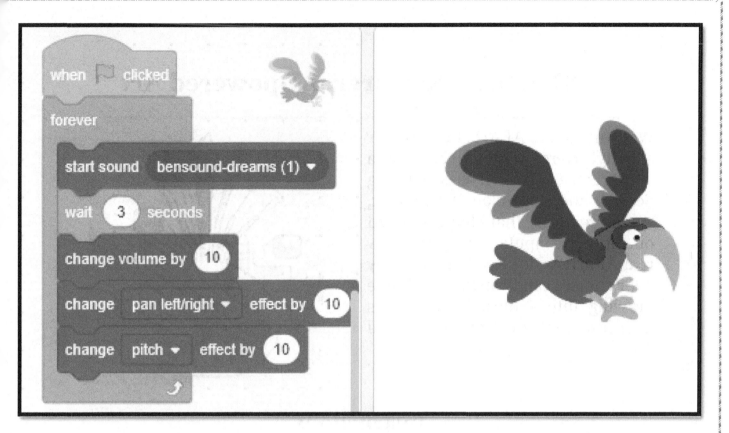

The Science Behind the Symphony Wizard

You're now a Digital Music Maestro:

🎵 You've learned how to tweak and play with sounds on a computer, just like professional sound engineers and music producers do!

Master of Randomness

🎲 You've seen how using random choices makes music unexpected and fun. This is a bit like how some AI in music works – it surprises us with new tunes!

Sound Wizardry Unlocked

🔊 You've got a taste of sound engineering by changing pitch and volume. In the big world, this is what helps make concerts sound epic and movies feel real.

Programming Power

🖥️ You've used programming to make your music interactive. This skill is super handy in making games, apps, and all sorts of cool digital tools that respond to what we do.

(8) Artistic Explorer: AI-powered Art

Welcome to the AI Artistic Explorer activity! Here, you will become a digital artist and an AI wizard. Using Scratch and a sprinkle of AI magic, you'll create art that changes based on different inputs – just like how real AI artists do! Ready to see how your choices can transform a simple drawing into a masterpiece? Let's dive into the world of AI-powered art!

Instructions

(1) Launch Your Scratch Project

» Go to **Scratch** and start a new project.

» Delete the default sprite by right-clicking on it and selecting 'delete'.

(2) Choose a Sprite for Your Artistic Explorer

» Click on '**Choose a Sprite**'.

» Pick a character that will be your AI Artistic Explorer.

(3) Start Programming

» Drag the "**when green flag clicked**" block from 'Events' category into the coding area.

» Drag "**set [color] effect to [0]**" block from the 'Looks' section to reset any previous color effects before asking the user for their color choice.

(4) Ask for Artistic Choices

» From the '**Sensing**' category, drag an "**ask [What color do you like? ("red", "blue", "green")] and wait**" block and attach it under your event block.

(5) Add Condition Statements

» Use "**if then**" blocks from the '**Control**' category to create different outcomes based on the answer. You will need three block for the three colors (i.e., red, blue, and green)

(6) Setup the Red Condition

» Inside the first "**if then**" block, add an "**=**" block from the '**Operators**' category.

» In the first slot of the "**=**" block, drag the "**answer**" block from the '**Sensing**' category. In the second slot, type "**red**".

» Inside the "**if then**", use a "**set [color] effect to [280]**" block from the '**Looks**' category.

(7) Setup the Blue Condition

» Repeat Step 6 for the color **blue**.

» In the "**if then**" condition, replace "**red**" with "blue" in the "**=**" block.

» Inside the "**if then**", use a "**set [color] effect to [180]**" block from the '**Looks**' category.

(8) Setup the Green Condition

» Again, repeat Step 6 for the color **green**.

» Change the "**=**" block to check if the answer is "**green**".

» Inside the "**if then**", use a "**set [color] effect to [0]**" block from the '**Looks**' category.

(9) Experiment with Color Values

» The effect of the color change depends on the original color of your sprite. You may need to experiment with different values to achieve the desired effect.

(10) Test Script and Save Your Project

» Run your script with different color inputs to see the effect of each color setting. This will help you fine-tune the values to get the colors you want.

» Save your creative AI art project by clicking 'File' and then 'Save now'.

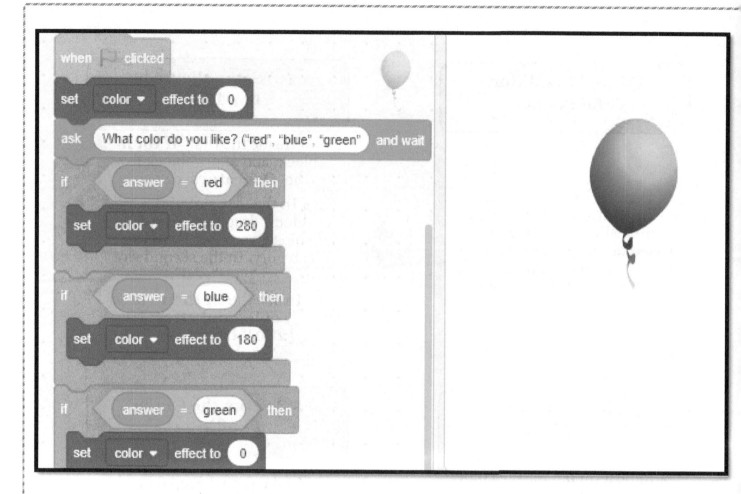

The Science Behind the AI-powered ART

Understanding AI and Creativity: You've just used basic programming to mimic how AI can create art. Real AI art systems analyze and use many art styles to make new creations!

Interactive Technology: Your project responds to user input, such as how interactive AI systems work in video games, apps, and digital art installations.

Digital Art: Artists use programs like Scratch and more advanced tools to create digital art, sometimes with AI adding its own twist.

Game Design: Your art-making experience responds to choices, resembling how designers create dynamic and responsive game environments.

User-Interactive Systems: Learning to program responses to user input is foundational in creating apps and systems that adapt to user preferences.

(9) AI Maze Navigator: The Maze Runner

Welcome to the AI Maze Navigator challenge! Ready to become a coding wizard and guide a robot through a twisting, turning maze? Using the power of Scratch and some clever programming, you'll create a robot that can find its way out of a maze, just like AI does in real-life navigation challenges. Let's gear up for this exciting adventure and see if your robot can make it to the finish line!

Instructions

(1) Launch Your Scratch Project

» Go to **Scratch** and start a new project.
» Delete the default sprite by right-clicking on it and selecting 'delete'.

(2) Choose a Sprite for Your Artistic Explorer

» Click on '**Choose a Sprite**'.
» Pick a character that will be your AI Maze Navigator.

(3) Set Up Your Maze

» Choose or draw a maze backdrop for your robot.
» You can create a maze using the backdrop drawing tools in Scratch or select a pre-made maze backdrop

(4) Start Programming

» From the '**Events**' category (yellow), drag a "**when green flag clicked**" block into your coding area.

(5) Set Up Your Maze

» Use blocks from the **'Motion'** category (blue) like **"move (10) steps"**, **"turn ↻ (15) degrees"**, **"change x by [value]"**, and **"change y by [value]"** to program your robot's movements.

(6) Start Programming

» Use the **"wait [0.5] seconds"** block in the **'Control'** category between the movement commands to watch the steps you programmed.

(7) Experiment with Mazes

» If you would like to use the same maze we used in the example, capture the maze and upload it to Scratch as a backdrop.

(8) Test Your Robot

» Click the green flag to start your program and watch how your robot navigates the maze.

» Observe and tweak your code based on where your robot gets stuck or makes wrong turns.

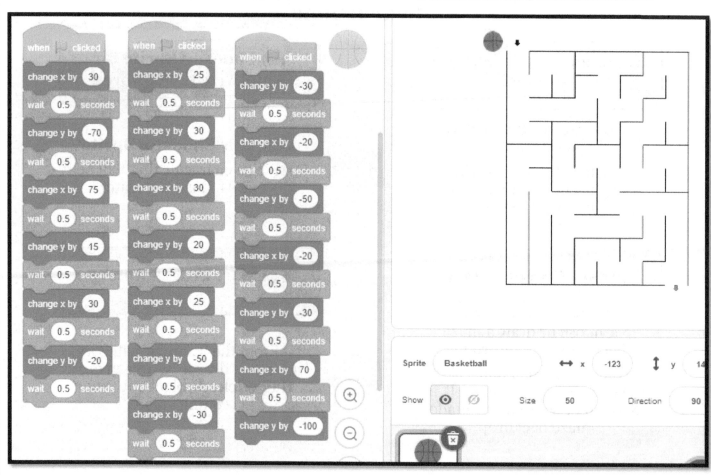

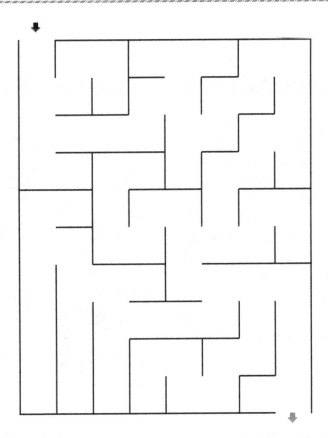

The Science Behind the AI Maze Navigator

Basic AI Concepts

You're learning about algorithms and decision-making, key components in AI. Your robot uses these to navigate the maze.

Problem-Solving

AI often involves solving problems step by step, just like navigating a maze. This is a fundamental skill in programming and robotics.

Sensing and Responding

Your robot uses 'sensing' to detect walls and 'control' to decide actions, similar to how real-world robots and AI systems interact with their environment.

Trial and Error Learning

You're practicing how AI systems often learn by testing and adjusting your code – by trying, failing, and improving.

(10) Fitness Adventure: AI-Led Excercises

Welcome to AI Fitness Adventure, where you become the leader of a fun and energetic exercise routine guided by AI! Imagine a world where your computer helps you stay active and healthy. In this exciting Scratch project, you'll program an AI coach that suggests different exercises and keeps you moving. Ready to jump, dance, and stretch your way into the world of fitness and technology?

Instructions

(1) Launch Your Scratch Project

» Go to **Scratch** and start a new project.
» Delete the default sprite by right-clicking on it and selecting 'delete'.

(2) Choose a Sprite for Your Artistic Explorer

» Click on '**Choose a Sprite**'.
» Pick a character that will be your AI Fitness Coach.

(3) Program the Warm-Up

» Drag a "**when green flag clicked**" block from the '**Events**' category (yellow) to start your routine.
» Use "**say [Let's get ready to exercise!] for [2] seconds**" from the '**Looks**' category (purple) to introduce the session.

(4) Set Up Exercise Options

» Use "**ask [What exercise should we start with? (jumping jacks, running in place, stretching)] and wait**" from the '**Sensing**' category (light blue) to engage users in choosing an exercise.

(5) Jumping Jacks Condition

» Drag an **"if then"** block from the '**Control**' category (orange) into your script.

» Inside this block, place an **"="** block from the '**Operators**' category (green). » In one slot, attach the **"answer"** block from '**Sensing**'. In the other slot, type **"jumping jacks"**.

(6) Jumping Jacks Command

» Within the **"if then"** block, use a combination of '**Looks**' and '**Sound**' blocks to simulate the AI Coach suggesting jumping jacks. For example:

"say [Let's do 10 jumping jacks!] for [2] seconds"

You could also add a sound or animation to visually represent the exercise, such as **"play sound [pop] until done"** from the '**Sound**' category, followed by **"wait [1] second"** from the '**Control**' category.

(7) Running in Place Condition

» Create another **"if then"** condition for "running in place".

» Use similar blocks as above, but change the text to suggest running in place. For example:

"say [Now, run in place for 30 seconds!] for [2] seconds"

(8) Stretching Condition

» Set up an **"if then"** condition for "stretching".

» In the **"if then"** block, program the AI Coach to suggest a simple stretching exercise. For example:

"say [Time to stretch! Reach up high and touch your toes.] for [3] seconds"

(9) Add a Loop for Continuous Exercise

» For each exercise, you can add a **"repeat (10)"** loop from the '**Control**' category around motion-related blocks to simulate doing the exercise several times.

(10) Cool Down

» After the exercise loop, add a cool-down message using the **"say [Great job! Time to cool down.]"** block.

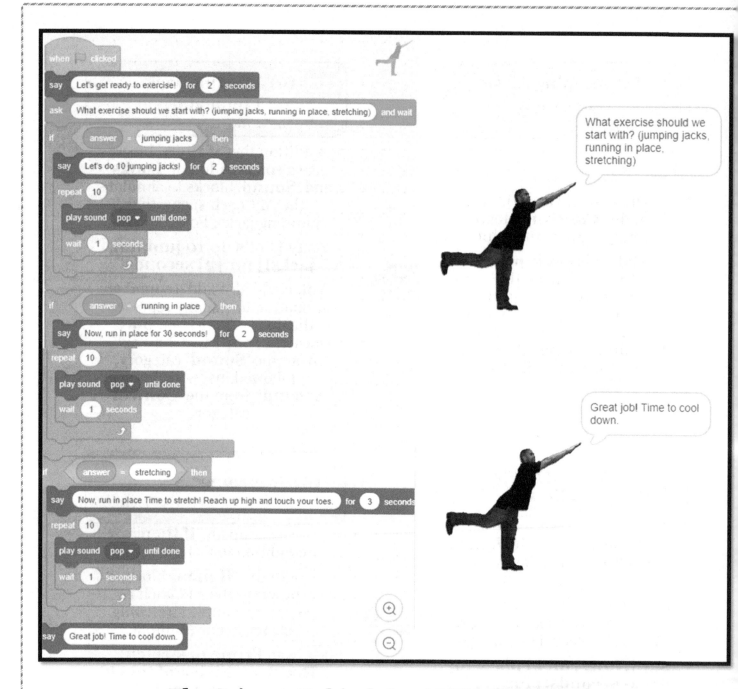

The Science Behind the AI Fitness Coach

Fitness Apps: Many fitness apps use AI to suggest workouts, track progress, and adapt routines to users' fitness levels.

Interactive Learning: This concept is used in educational games and apps where children are encouraged to participate in physical activities through interactive prompts.

Health and Wellness Tech: From smartwatches to virtual trainers, AI plays a big role in modern fitness and health monitoring.

(11) AI Memory Maestro Challenge

Welcome to the AI Memory Maestro challenge! Get ready to boost your brain power with a fun memory game where AI creates challenging sequences for you to remember. Using Scratch, you'll build a game that tests and improves your memory skills. Watch as the AI randomly generates sequences of colors or sounds, and see how many you can recall. Are you ready to become a Memory Maestro?

Instructions

(1) Launch Your Scratch Project

» Go to **Scratch** and start a new project.

» Delete the default sprite by right-clicking on it and selecting 'delete'.

(2) Design the Game Interface

» Choose a backdrop that fits the theme of a memory game (we uploaded a brain backdrop)

(3) Select the Main Control Sprite

» Select one sprite to act as your **'Control Sprite'**. This sprite will manage the game (We chose a **Parrot** as a Control Sprite)

(4) Select 4 Additional Sprites

» Choose or create four additional sprites that will be part of the memory sequence.

» These could be different colored shapes, objects, or animals (We chose a **Cat, a Dog, a Horse, and a Rooster**)

(5) Assign Sounds to Each Sprite

» Click on each of the four sprites individually to add sounds.

» Go to the '**Sounds**' tab in the upper area of the Scratch interface.

» Click on the '**Choose a Sound**' icon (looks like a speaker) to select a sound from the library or upload your own.

» Ensure each of these four sprites has a distinct sound assigned.

(6) Programming the Control Sprite

» Click on your **Control Sprite**.

» Drag a "**when green flag clicked**" block from the '**Events**' category to start the game.

» Create a new variable named "**Sequence**" for all sprites. This is done by clicking on '**Variables**' > '**Make a Variable**'.

» Inside the control sprite's script, add a "**forever**" loop from the '**Control**' category.

(7) Random Sequence Generation

» Inside the "**forever**" loop, place a "**set [Sequence] to (pick random (1) to (4))**" block from the '**Variables**' and '**Operators**' categories, respectively.

» Still within the loop, add an "**if then**" statement for each possible value of "**Sequence**". Use the block "**Sequence**" from the '**Variables**' category for "**if then**" conditions.

(8) Broadcast Messages Based on Sequence

» For each value (1, 2, 3, 4), use a "**broadcast [sprite1Action, sprite2Action, etc.]**" block from the '**Events**' category.

» Ensure there's a small wait time after each broadcast to prevent overlap.

(9) Reacting to Broadcast

» For each of your four action sprites, create a script that reacts to its corresponding broadcast.

» Use a **"when I receive [spriteXAction]"** block followed by **"play sound [sound name]"** from the '**Events**' and '**Sound**' categories, respectively.

(10) Test Player Memory

» After the sequence is played, ask the player to recall the sequence.

» Use the **"ask [Which sprite played the sound?] and wait"** block from the '**Sensing**' category on the **control sprite**.

The Science Behind the AI Memory Maestro Game

Memory and Brain Exercise

Just like muscles, your brain gets stronger when you exercise it. Playing memory games is a great way to train your brain, improving your memory and attention skills.

Pattern Recognition

The game helps you practice pattern recognition, which is noticing and understanding patterns or sequences. It's an essential skill in everyday life and complex tasks like math and science.

Programming Logic

When you programmed the game, you used logical thinking to tell the computer what to do. This is a big part of coding – giving clear instructions so the computer can perform tasks correctly.

Real-World Applications

Educational Software: Memory games in educational apps use similar concepts to help kids learn in a fun way.

AI in Real Life: AI systems use pattern recognition and randomness in recommending videos on YouTube, helping scientists analyze data, or even self-driving cars.

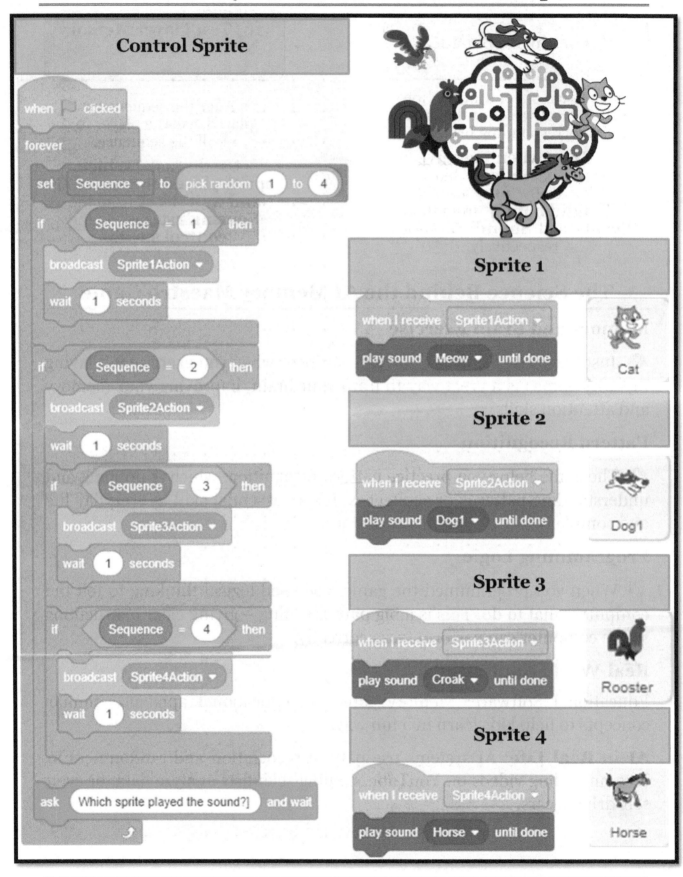

Control Sprite

```
when [flag] clicked
forever
  set Sequence ▾ to (pick random (1) to (4))
  if < Sequence = (1) > then
    broadcast Sprite1Action ▾
    wait (1) seconds
  if < Sequence = (2) > then
    broadcast Sprite2Action ▾
    wait (1) seconds
  if < Sequence = (3) > then
    broadcast Sprite3Action ▾
    wait (1) seconds
  if < Sequence = (4) > then
    broadcast Sprite4Action ▾
    wait (1) seconds
  ask [Which sprite played the sound?] and wait
```

Sprite 1

```
when I receive Sprite1Action ▾
play sound Meow ▾ until done
```

Cat

Sprite 2

```
when I receive Sprite2Action ▾
play sound Dog1 ▾ until done
```

Dog1

Sprite 3

```
when I receive Sprite3Action ▾
play sound Croak ▾ until done
```

Rooster

Sprite 4

```
when I receive Sprite4Action ▾
play sound Horse ▾ until done
```

Horse

(12) AI Shark Snack Quest

Get ready for an adventure with AI Monster Munchies! In this fun and interactive game, you'll create a lovable monster with a big appetite. But there's a twist – your monster has particular food preferences, and it's up to you to feed it the right snacks! Using Scratch, you'll program the monster to ask for different foods and then respond to your choices. Let's dive into the world of coding and see if you can keep your monster happy and well-fed!

Instructions

(1) Launch Your Scratch Project

» Go to **Scratch** and start a new project.

» Delete the default sprite by right-clicking on it and selecting 'delete'.

(2) Create Your Shark

» Choose a shark sprite from Scratch's library or draw your own.

» Position your shark sprite in an ocean-themed backdrop.

(3) Set Up the Food Choices

» Add sprites for the shark's snacks: apples, bananas, strawberries, and tacos.

Arrange them around the stage.

(4) Create a Variable for Random Food Selection

» Make a new variable named **"FoodChoice"** for all sprites by clicking on '**Variables**' > '**Make a Variable**'.

(5) Start Programming the Shark

» In the **shark sprite**, start with a "**when green flag clicked**" block from the 'Events' category.

» Add a "**forever**" loop from the '**Control**' category to keep the game going.

» Inside the loop, use "**ask [Which snack should I give?] and wait**" from the 'Sensing' category.

(6) Program the Shark to Choose a Food

» Inside the loop, set "**FoodChoice**" to a random number between 1 and 4 using the "**set [FoodChoice] to (pick random (1) to (4))**" block.

» Use "**if then**" statements to display different messages based on the value of "**FoodChoice**" (e.g., "**if <(FoodChoice) = [1]> then say [I want an apple!]** for [2] seconds").

» Use the block "**FoodChoice**" from the '**Variables**' category for "**if then**" conditions.

(7) Start Feeding the Shark

» Ask a player to choose a food and check if the player's response matches the "**FoodChoice**".

(8) Play with Multiple Players

» You can have multiple players and check who wins in several rounds!

The Science Behind the AI Shark Snack Quest

Randomization in AI: This activity demonstrates how AI can make random choices, similar to how algorithms in games and apps sometimes decide what happens next.

Variables in Programming: Learning to use variables is a fundamental skill in coding. They help keep track of information like the shark's food choice.

Conditional Logic: Using "if-then" statements is essential to programming logic, allowing for different outcomes based on certain conditions.

Game Design: Skills learned here apply to creating interactive games where players' choices affect the gameplay.

(13) AI Color Lab

Welcome to the AI Color Lab! Get ready to become a color scientist and explore the fascinating world of colors. In this magical experiment, you'll use primary colors – red, blue, and yellow – to create a whole spectrum of new colors. Using Scratch, you'll program an AI assistant that helps mix these colors and discover the results. Let's dive into the colorful adventure and see what amazing hues you can create!

Instructions

(1) Launch Your Scratch Project

» Go to **Scratch** and start a new project.

» Delete the default sprite by right-clicking on it and selecting 'delete'.

(2) Set Up Color Sprites

» Choose or create sprites for the primary colors: red, blue, and yellow.

» Position these color sprites on the stage.

» Use a plain white backdrop where the mixed colors will be shown.

(3) Program the AI Assistant

» Select or create a sprite to act as your AI Color Assistant.

» Start with a **"when green flag clicked"** block from the '**Events**' category.

» Add a "**forever**" loop from the '**Control**' category.

(4) Ask for Color Choices

» Inside the loop, use "**ask [Which two primary colors should we mix?] and wait**" from the '**Sensing**' category.

» This block allows users to input their choices of two colors to mix.

(5) Using Conditional Logic for Color Mixing

» Inside the "**forever**" loop, after the "**ask and wait**" block, use "**if then**" blocks to check for specific color combinations.

» The player will input two primary colors, and you need to program the AI assistant to recognize these combinations and create the appropriate mixed color.

(6) Set Your Backdrop Colors

» Ensure you have backdrops corresponding to each mixed color (**purple, orange, green**).

» If Scratch doesn't have a backdrop in the exact color you need (**purple, orange, or green**), you can upload or create one.

(7) Create Your Backdrop colors

» Click on the '**Choose a Backdrop**' button (paintbrush icon) and select a plain backdrop (like a white backdrop).

» Then, use the '**Fill**' tool to change its color to match the color you need.

» Name each backdrop according to its color for easy reference in your code (e.g., 'Purple', 'Orange', 'Green').

(8) Displaying the Resulting Color

» Use a series of "**if then**" blocks from the '**Control**' category to create different color outcomes based on the player's input.

» In each "**if then**" block, use "**switch backdrop to [color]**" from the 'Looks' category to change the stage's backdrop to the mixed color.

(9) Program Your Conditions

» if <(**answer**) = [**red and blue**]> then switch backdrop to [**Purple**]

» if <(**answer**) = [**red and yellow**]> then switch backdrop to [**Orange**]

» if <(**answer**) = [**blue and yellow**]> then switch backdrop to [**Green**]

(10) Experiment with More Colors

Experiment with different color combinations and add more "if then" conditions to represents each combination.

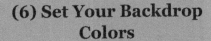

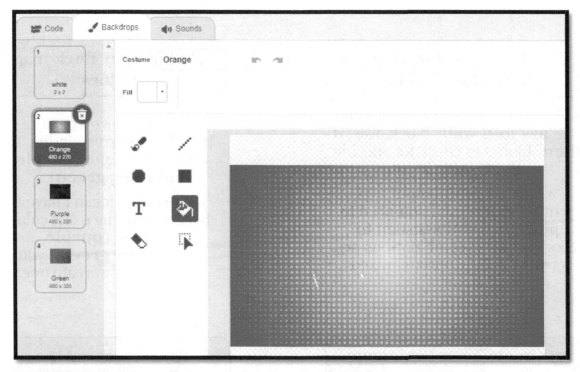

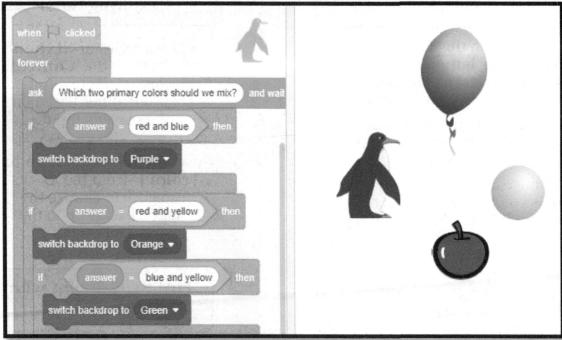

The Science Behind the AI Color Lab

Real-World Applications

Digital Art and Design: Understanding color mixing is fundamental in digital art, graphic design, and animation.

Educational Software: Educational software uses Similar interactive activities to teach children about colors and art.

(14) AI Space Mission

Welcome aboard the AI Space Mission! Get ready for an epic journey through the stars. As the commander of a space mission, you'll be assisted by an AI to navigate the vastness of space. Using Scratch, you'll simulate a thrilling space adventure where AI helps guide your spaceship to different planets and galaxies. Prepare for liftoff, and let's explore the mysteries of the universe with our AI co-pilot!

Instructions

(1) Begin Your Scratch Space Journey

» Go to **Scratch** and start a new project.
» Delete the default sprite by right-clicking on it and selecting 'delete'.

(2) Set Up Your Spacecraft and AI Assistant

» Choose a spacecraft sprite and an AI character sprite, like a robot or a futuristic computer.
» Select a space-themed backdrop or create one. You can start with a backdrop of Earth.

(3) Program the Spacecraft's Takeoff

» Click on your spacecraft sprite.
» Drag a "**when green flag clicked**" block from the '**Events**' category.

(4) Create a List of Planets to Explore

» Make a list named "**Planets**" in the '**Variables**' section.
» Add names of planets like **Mars**, **Jupiter**, **Saturn**, etc., to the list.

(5) AI Asks Where to Go Next

» Add a "**forever**" loop from the '**Control**' category.

» Inside the loop, use "**ask [Which planet shall we visit next? Mars, Jupiter, or Saturn?] and wait**" from the '**Sensing**' category.

» This allows players to choose a planet to explore.

(6) Prepare Your Backdrops

» Ensure that you have backdrops for **Mars, Jupiter, and Saturn**.

» Go to the '**Backdrops**' tab near the stage area.

» You can either choose suitable backdrops from Scratch's library, create your own, or upload ones. Name them accordingly (e.g., 'Mars', 'Jupiter', 'Saturn').

(7) Set Up Conditional Statements

» Use "**if then**" statements to check the player's response and switch the backdrop accordingly using "**switch backdrop to [Planet]**" from the '**Looks**' category

» Compare the player's answer to each planet name using equal-to "**=**" operators from the '**Operators**' category.

(8) Programming the Responses

» **For Mars**: if <(answer) = [Mars]> then switch backdrop to [Mars]

» **For Jupiter**: if <(answer) = [Jupiter]> then switch backdrop to [Jupiter]

» **For Saturn**: if <(answer) = [Saturn]> then switch backdrop to [Saturn]

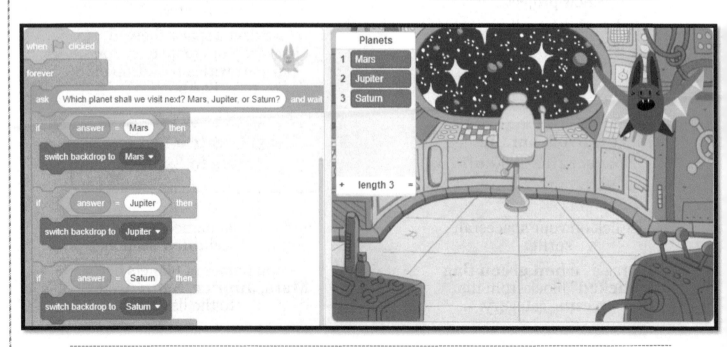

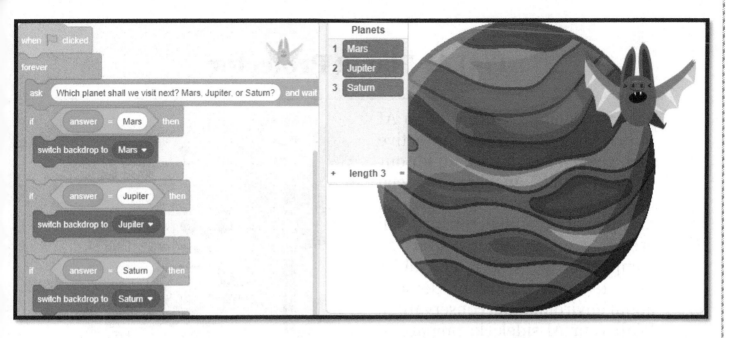

The Science Behind the AI Space Mission

Astronomy and Space Exploration

Explore the characteristics of different planets, enhancing knowledge about our solar system.

AI and Decision-Making

Understand how AI can assist in navigation and make decisions based on user input.

Programming Interactive Experiences

Develop skills in creating engaging and interactive programs that respond to user choices.

Real-World Applications

Space Missions

AI technology is crucial in real space missions, aiding in navigation and data analysis.

Educational Software

Techniques used here are similar to those in educational apps, teaching kids about space in an engaging way.

(15) AI Planet Protector

Embark on an adventure as an AI Planet Protector! In this interactive game, you'll become a hero for our environment, making crucial decisions to recycle and care for our planet. Using Scratch, you'll create a game where your AI companion helps sort recyclables and teaches important lessons about environmental conservation. With your AI sidekick, prepare to save the planet, one recyclable at a time!

Instructions

(1) Launch Your Scratch Environmental Mission

» Go to **Scratch** and start a new project.
» Delete the default sprite by right-clicking on it and selecting 'delete'.

(2) Set Up Your Game Environment

» Create a backdrop that resembles an environment-friendly setting, like a park or a recycling center.

(3) Create an AI Helper Sprite

» Select or design an AI character sprite, such as a robot or a wise tree, that will assist in sorting the recyclables.

(4) Create Backdrops for Each Item

» You can display different recyclable items by changing the backdrop. Find images or create simple drawings of the following items:
» **A piece of paper**.
» **A soda can**.
» **A plastic bottle**.

(5) Upload the Images to Scratch

» Go to the "**Choose a backdrop from file**" option to upload the images you created.

» Name the backdrop with the paper image as "**Paper,**" the backdrop with the can image as "**Can,**" and the backdrop with the bottle image as "**Bottle.**"

(6) Start Programming the Game

» Click on your AI sprite.

» Use a "**when green flag clicked**" block from the '**Events**' category to begin the game.

» Add a "**forever**" loop from the '**Control**' category.

» Insert the "**next backdrop**" block from the "Looks" category. This block will automatically change the backdrop to the next one in your list of backdrops every time the loop runs.

(7) Ask for Player Interaction

» Add a "wait [10]seconds" block from the '**Control**' category after changing the backdrop. This gives players a moment to see the new backdrop before responding.

» Within the forever loop, insert an "**ask [What should we do with this item? Recycle or Trash?] and wait**" block from the '**Sensing**' category. This block prompts the player to make a decision about recycling.

(8) Use "if-then-else" Condition

» Follow the "**ask and wait**" block with an **if-then-else** condition from the "**Control**" and "**Operators**" categories.

» Inside the "**if**" condition, use an "**and**" operator block from the "**Operators**" category. This operator will allow you to check two conditions simultaneously: the current backdrop and the player's answer.

(9) Teach the AI Assistant to Recognize backdrops

» You'll need to get the current backdrop's name. For this, use the "**backdrop name**" block from the "**Looks**" category.

» Attach the "**backdrop name**" block to one side of the "=" operator. In the other part of the "=" operator, type the name of the backdrop you want to check against, for example, "**Can**".

(10) Complete the "if-then-else" Conditions

The condition in the "**if**" block will look like:

» If (backdrop name [Paper] and answer [Recycle]) then "say [Correct! Good job!] for [2] seconds." Else, "say [Oops! That's not right. Let's try again!] for [2] seconds."

» You will need to create a similar set of if-then-else statements for each backdrop (**Can, Bottle, etc.**).

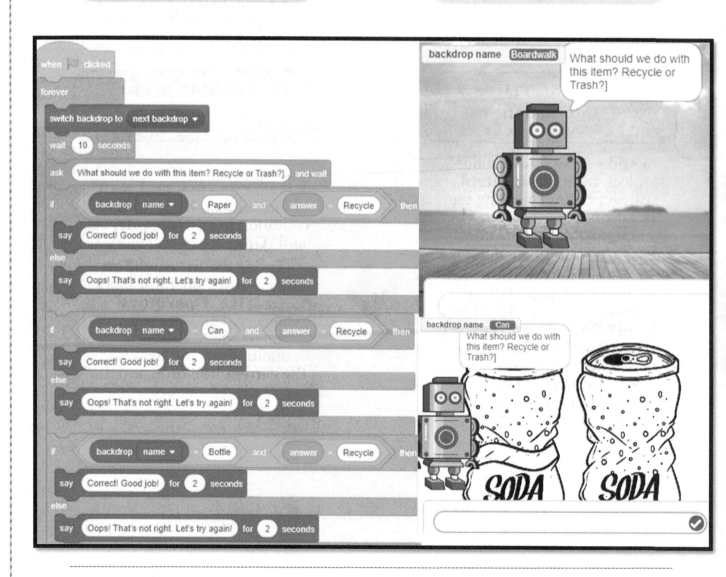

(16) AI Emoji Magic: Craft Your Emotions

Welcome to "AI Emoji Magic: Craft Your Emotions!" a fun-filled, creative adventure where you become an emoji wizard! Using the magic of coding in Scratch, you'll create a tool that brings emojis to life with your own expressive twists. Imagine crafting a smiley that winks or a surprised face that really jumps out! This journey isn't just about fun; it's a first step into the world of AI and digital expression. Ready to start your journey into the art of emoji creation? Let's go!

Instructions

(1) Launch Your Scratch Emoji Fun

» Go to **Scratch** and start a new project.

» Delete the default sprite by right-clicking on it and selecting 'delete'.

(2) Add Emoji and AI Chat Sprites

» Click "**Choose a Sprite**" and select or upload emoji images. Start with basic faces – **happy, sad, surprised**.

» Add a sprite to represent your AI chat robot

(3) Action for Each Emoji Sprite

» For the three Emoji sprites, drag "**when green flag clicked**" from "**Events.**"

» Add "**hide**" from "**Looks**" to make the sprite invisible at the start.

(4) Program Your AI to Ask Questions

» In the AI sprite's script, add "**when green flag clicked**" from "**Events.**"

Use "**ask [How do you feel today: happy, sad, or surprised?] and wait**" from "**Sensing.**"

(5) Script AI Robot's Responses

» Use "**if...then**" blocks from "**Control**" for each emotion.

» Within each, check the player's response using "**equals**" blocks from "**Operators**" and the "**answer**" block from "**Sensing**."

(6) If-Then Conditions

» Use "**broadcast [happy/sad/surprised]**" from "**Events**" inside the respective "**if...then**" statements.

» if <(answer) = [happy]> then broadcast [happy]

» if <(answer) = [sad]> then broadcast [sad]

» if <(answer) = [surprised]> then broadcast [surprised]

(7) Script Emoji Sprite Actions

Action for Happy Sprite:

Use "**when I receive [happy]**" from "**Events.**" Attach "**show**" from "**Looks**"

Action for Sad Sprite:

Use "**when I receive [sad]**" from "**Events.**" Attach "**show**" from "**Looks**"

Action for Surprised Sprite:

Use "**when I receive [surprised]**" from "**Events.**" Attach "**show**" from "**Looks**"

(8) If-Then Conditions

» Run your project, test interactions, and refine the scripts as needed.

» Repeat the steps to include more emoji expressions.

» Share your game with others for feedback and fun.

How do you feel today: happy, sad, or surprised?

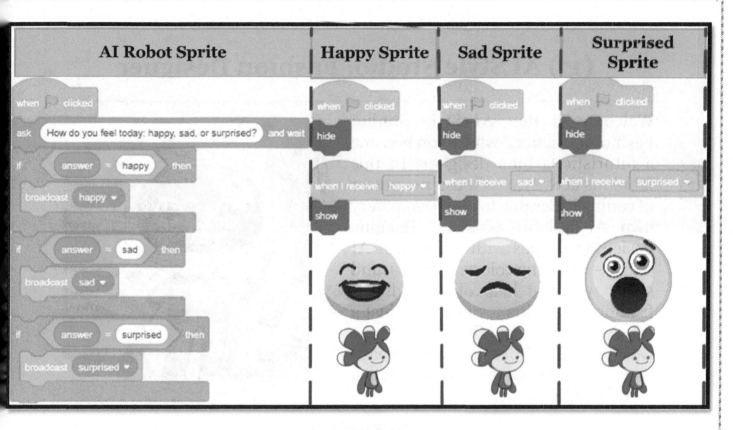

AI Robot Sprite	Happy Sprite	Sad Sprite	Surprised Sprite
when ⚑ clicked	when ⚑ clicked	when ⚑ clicked	when ⚑ clicked
ask How do you feel today: happy, sad, or surprised? and wait	hide	hide	hide
if answer = happy then	when I receive happy ▾	when I receive sad ▾	when I receive surprised ▾
broadcast happy ▾	show	show	show
if answer = sad then			
broadcast sad ▾			
if answer = surprised then			
broadcast surprised ▾			

The Science Behind the AI Emoji Magic

Emotional Recognition

Understand how AI can identify and respond to human emotions.

Basic Programming Skills

Develop skills in logical thinking and programming through if-then statements and loops.

Real-World Application

This activity mimics real-world AI applications in games, virtual assistants, and educational software that respond to user inputs.

Importance

Grasping the basics of AI and programming through this activity can spark interest in technology, coding, and emotional intelligence.

(17) AI Style Studio: Fashion Designer

Welcome to the "AI Style Studio: Fashion Designer," where you become a futuristic fashion designer! In this fabulous activity, you'll use the power of coding in Scratch to create your very own AI fashion assistant. Imagine designing clothes with a touch of AI magic – selecting colors, patterns, and styles with the help of your digital fashion guru. This is more than just a fun exercise; it's your first step into the world of AI and design. Let's unleash your creativity and dive into the stylish world of AI fashion!

Instructions

(1) Launch Your Scratch Style Studio Project

» Go to **Scratch** and start a new project.
» Delete the default sprite by right-clicking on it and selecting 'delete'.

(2) Add Your AI Fashion Assistant

» Add a sprite that will represent your AI fashion assistant. This could be a robot, a mannequin, or any character you like.

(3) Design Fashion Items

» Go to **"Costumes"** tab for your sprite.
» Create, edit, or upload costumes to represent a dress in three colors: **red, black, and green**. Name them appropriately like **"Red Dress," "Black Dress," "Green Dress."**

(4) Program Your AI

» Use **"when green flag clicked"** from "Events."
» Follow with **"ask [Which dress color do you like? Red, Black, or Green?] and wait"** from "Sensing."

(5) Set Your Conditions

» Use "**if...then**" blocks to change the dress color based on the answer.

Check the player's response using "**equals**" blocks and the "**answer**" block.

(6) If-Then Statements

» if <(answer) = [red]> then switch costume to [Red Dress]

» if <(answer) = [black]> then switch costume to [Black Dress]

» if <(answer) = [green]> then switch costume to [Green Dress]

The Science Behind the AI Style Studio

AI in Creative Choices: Understand how AI can assist in making creative decisions like choosing dress colors.

Programming Skills: Develop skills in conditional logic and event handling.

Applications:

Fashion and AI: AI is increasingly used in the fashion industry for tasks like trend forecasting and personalized recommendations.

Creative AI: AI tools are aiding artists and designers in exploring new creative possibilities.

(18) AI Zoo Explorer: Wild World Classifier

Welcome to the "AI Zoo Explorer: Wild World Classifier," an exciting journey into the animal kingdom with the help of AI! In this adventure, you'll become a young AI scientist, creating a tool that classifies animals based on different characteristics like their habitat, size, and diet. It's not just fun – you're stepping into the world of AI and learning about how it helps us make sense of the world around us. Let's embark on this wild exploration and discover the amazing diversity of animal life!

Instructions

(1) Launch Your Scratch AI Zoo Explorer Project

» Go to **Scratch** and start a new project.

» Delete the default sprite by right-clicking on it and selecting 'delete'.

(2) Add Your Sprites

» Add sprites **for a bird, a fish, and a lion**. You can find these in Scratch's sprite library or upload your own images.

» Add a sprite that will act as your AI classifier, such as a robot or a computer.

(3) Set Up Your Animal Sprites

» For the Bird, Fish, and Lion sprites Add a "**when green flag clicked**" block from the "**Events**" followed by a "**hide**" block from the "**Looks**" for each animal sprite.

(4) Set Up Your AI Assistant Sprite

» Add "**when green flag clicked**" from "**Events**" followed by "**ask [Does it fly, swim, or walk?] and wait**" from "**Sensing**."

(5) Classifying Based on Answers

» Use conditional statements **"if-then"** from **"Control"** to classify the animals.

» Use **"broadcast [message]"** from **"Events"** to broadcast messages like "show bird," "show fish," or "show lion" based on the answer

(6) If-Then Statements

» if <(answer) = [fly]> then broadcast [show bird]

» if <(answer) = [swim]> then broadcast [show fish]

» if <(answer) = [walk]> then broadcast [show lion]

(7) Add Scripts for Bird and Fish Sprites

» Hide the Bird, Fish, and Lion sprites using **"when green flag clicked"** from **"Events"** followed by **"hide"** from **"Looks."**

» Add **"when I receive [show bird]"** from **"Events"** to the Bird sprite.

» Add **"when I receive [show fish]"** from **"Events."**

» Add a **"show"** block from **"Looks"** to the Fish sprite.

(8) Add Script for Lion Sprite and Test your AI Classifier

» Add **"when I receive [show lion]"** from **"Events"** to the Lion sprite.

» Add a **"show"** block from **"Looks"** to the Bird, Fish, and Lion sprites.

» Test your AI animal classifier, make any necessary tweaks, and then share it with friends or the Scratch community.

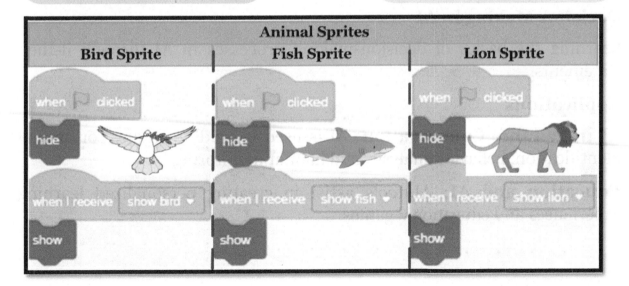

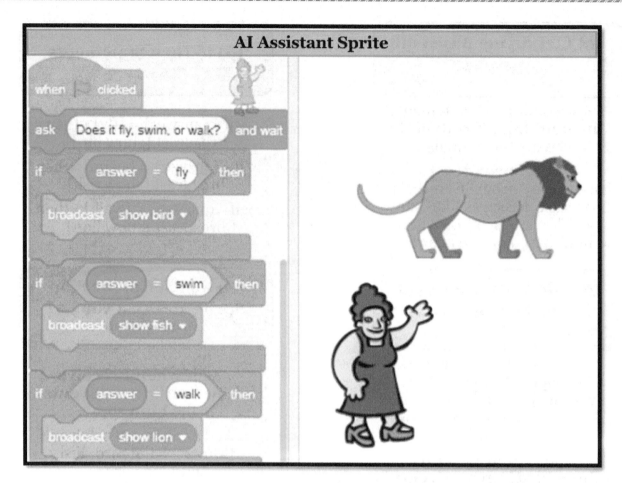

The Science Behind the AI Zoo Explorer

Categorization in AI

Understanding how AI uses characteristics to categorize and classify data, mimicking how human brains categorize information.

Decision-Making in AI

Learning the basics of decision-making processes in AI through if-then statements.

Applications

AI in Wildlife Conservation: AI is used in wildlife studies for animal identification, behavior analysis, and habitat monitoring.

Education and AI: AI tools assist in creating personalized learning experiences and educational games.

(19) AI Home Commander: Interactive Living

Welcome to "AI Home Commander: Smart Living"! Imagine stepping into a home where everything responds to your touch or voice – lights dim, music plays, and doors open as if by magic. This isn't just a fantasy; it's the smart home of the future, and you're going to create it! Using Scratch, you'll program an AI to control a virtual house, learning about automation and the amazing potential of AI in our daily lives. Ready to become an architect of the future? Let's start building your smart home!

Instructions

(1) Launch Your AI Home Commander Project

» Go to **Scratch** and start a new project.

» Delete the default sprite by right-clicking on it and selecting 'delete'.

(2) Designing Your Smart Home

» Create or choose a backdrop that represents the inside of a home.

» Add three sprites representing the smart devices: **Lights, Speakers, and Doors**.

(3) Add AI Control Sprite

» Add a sprite that will represent your AI home commander, like a smart tablet or a friendly robot.

(4) Ask for User Input

» Use **"when green flag clicked"** from "Events" to start the interaction.

» Use **"ask ["Which device should I control? Lights, Speakers, or Doors?"] and wait"** from **"Sensing"** to inquire which device to control.

(5) AI Assistant Responds to User Input

» Use "**if...then**" blocks from "**Control**" to create conditions for each device.

» Use "**broadcast [message]**" from "**Events**" to send commands to the specific device sprites.

(6) If-Then Statements

» if <(answer) = [lights]> then broadcast [control lights]

» if <(answer) = [speakers]> then broadcast [control speakers]

» if <(answer) = [doors]> then broadcast [control doors]

(7) Add Scripts for Lights and Speakers Sprites

» Hide the Lights, Speakers, and Doors sprite using "**when green flag clicked**" from "**Events**" followed by "**hide**" block from "**Looks.**"

» Add "**when I receive [control lights]**" from "**Events**" to the Lights sprite.

» Add "**when I receive [control speakers]**" from "**Events**" to the Speakers sprite.

(8) Add Script for Doors Sprite and Test your AI Home Commander

» Add "**when I receive [control doors]**" from "**Events**" to the Doors sprite.

» Add a "**show**" block from "**Looks.**"

» Add a "**show**" block from "**Looks**" the Lights, Speakers, and Doors sprite

» Test your AI Home Commander, Add more detailed commands or scenarios like "dim lights" or "play jazz music."

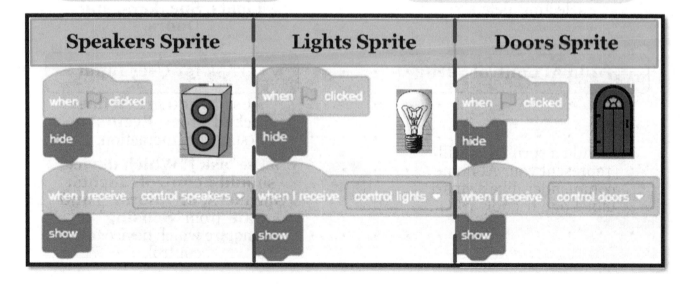

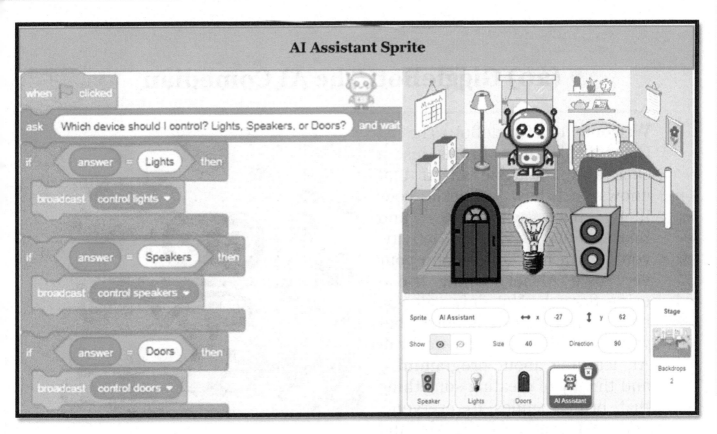

The Science Behind the AI Home Commander

Automation and Control Systems

Automation involves the creation of technology to control and monitor the production and delivery of various goods and services. In the context of a smart home, this means controlling lighting, temperature, entertainment systems, and security systems.

The Role of AI in Home Automation

AI can learn from user behaviors and automate actions based on patterns. For instance, an AI might learn at what time of day a user prefers dimmed lights or what kind of music they like to listen to when they get home.

Real-World Impact

By understanding the science behind these systems, you can appreciate the real-world applications of AI and automation in creating efficient, safe, and comfortable living environments.

(20) GiggleBot: The AI Comedian

Welcome to "GiggleBot: The AI Comedian," where fun is just a click away! Imagine an AI that knows just how to tickle your funny bone with jokes and hilarious stories. In this activity, you'll learn how to program your very own AI joke-telling friend using Scratch. Not only will you have a blast hearing its jokes, but you'll also dive into the world of AI, learning about programming and the joy of creating something that brings smiles to everyone. Let's get ready to chuckle and code!

Instructions

(1) Launch Your AI Comedian Project

» Go to **Scratch** and start a new project.

» Delete the default sprite by right-clicking on it and selecting 'delete'.

(2) Adding Your AI Jokester Sprite

» Create or choose a backdrop that represents a stage for your Jokester sprite.

» Add a sprite that will represent your AI Jokester, like a robot or a whimsical character.

(3) Start Programming

» Drag the "**when green flag clicked**" block from "**Events**" to start your program.

» Use a "**forever**" loop from "**Control**" to continuously offer jokes.

(4) Ask the User

» Use the "**ask [Want to hear a funny joke?] and wait**" block from "**Sensing**" to ask if the user wants to hear a joke.

(5) AI Comedian Responds to User Input

» Use "**if...then...else**" statements from "**Control**" to decide whether to tell a joke based on the user's response.

» Program the AI to tell two different jokes using "say" blocks from "**Control**". After each joke, use a "**play sound [ ] until done**" block to play a laughter track to simulate an audience's reaction.

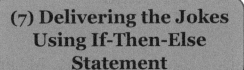

(6) Delivering the Jokes

» Click on the "**Sounds**" tab next to the "**Code**" tab.

» Click on the speaker icon (Choose a Sound) at the bottom-left corner of the screen.

» Browse through the sounds under categories like "**Human**" or "**Funny**."

» Select a laughter sound effect, such as "**Crowd Laugh**" and click "**OK**" to add it to your project.

(7) Delivering the Jokes Using If-Then-Else Statement

» if <(answer) = [yes]> then say [Why don't scientists trust atoms? Because they make up everything!] for 10 secs.

» play sound [Crowd Laugh] until done.

» say [What did one wall say to the other wall? I'll meet you at the corner!] for 10 secs

» play sound [Crowd Laugh] until done

» else say [Alright, let me know when you're ready!] for 2 secs.

(8) Testing your AI Jokester and Adding More Jokes

» Test your GiggleBot by interacting with it, listening to the jokes, and adjusting timing or effects as needed.

» Add options for the user to continue listening to jokes or end the interaction, enhancing user engagement and replay value.

» Add more "**say**" and "**play sound**" blocks for additional jokes, creating a variety of humorous interactions. Consider using the "**pick random**" block from "**Operators**" to randomly select jokes from a list.

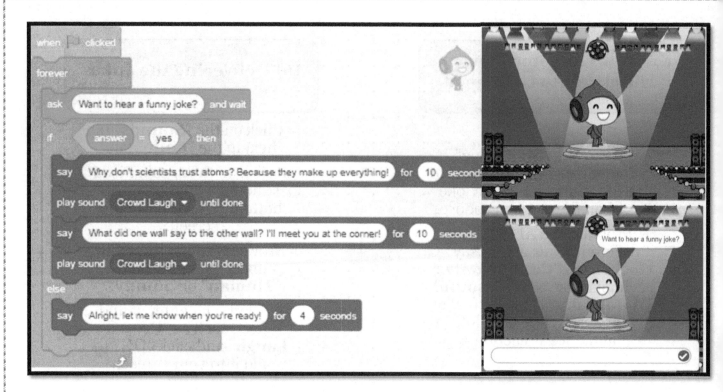

The Science Behind the AI Comedian

Creative Computing

AI is not just about data and algorithms; it's also a tool for creativity. AI can generate jokes, stories, and even art, pushing the boundaries of traditional computing.

Algorithms and Patterns

Behind every joke or story, the AI follows a pattern or algorithm to deliver content that makes sense and follows a logical structure.

Emotional Intelligence and AI

For AI to be effective, especially in entertainment, it must understand and sometimes emulate human emotions. A joke is more than just words; it's about delivery, timing, and understanding what makes humans laugh.

Applications and Implications

By engaging with an AI comedian, you see the entertaining side of AI and its potential in education, therapy, and more personalized user experiences. You start to appreciate the complexity behind seemingly simple interactions and consider how AI might fit into different aspects of life.

FUTURE AI EXPERT

Future SmartMinds

www.futuresmartminds.com

Welcome to the **FutureSmartMinds** family!

Thank you for choosing **"Future AI Expert: A Journey into the Exciting World of Artificial Intelligence"** from our **STEM Explorers Series: Ignite the Future**. Your decision to bring this adventure into your home or classroom is the first step in joining a wonderful journey of discovery and innovation that spans the captivating world of STEM (Science, Technology, Engineering, and Mathematics).

We kindly invite you to share your thoughts about **"Future AI Expert"** on Amazon. Your feedback helps us continue to improve and inspire more young minds. Your honest review will guide others in making their choice and encourage them to join us in shaping the future of our future smart minds.

Scan to Rate Us on Amazon

Once again, thank you for being a part of our FutureSmartMinds community. We're excited to have you with us on this journey.

Warm regards,

The **FutureSmartMinds** Team

www.futuresmartminds.com

Email: FutureSmartMindsKids@gmail.com

 @futuresmartminds

 @futuresmartminds

 @ futuresmartminds

Scan to visit our website

Please check our other kids' **STEM** activities books!

Available on Amazon!

(Scan the QR code to visit Amazon store)

Introduce your child to the captivating world of engineering." This exceptional book is tailored for budding young minds, ages 7 to 12, and is brimming with astonishing STEM engineering experiments that ignite creativity and critical thinking.

Unleash Engineering Wonders: Engineering is all around us, but sometimes it can seem complex. "**Future Engineer**" bridges this gap by unveiling mind-blowing engineering experiments that use everyday household items, making engineering accessible, exciting, and hands-on. These experiments spark curiosity and develop analytical skills.

Available on Amazon!

(Scan the QR code to visit our Amazon store)

Prepare for an exciting journey into the world of science! Our book is designed to captivate young minds, ages 7 to 12, with engaging experiments that uncover the magic of scientific concepts. These experiments unravel unpredictable phenomena, demonstrating that science explains the unexplained.

Unlock the World of Science: Science is all around us, and we've crafted mind-blowing experiments using everyday household items to demystify its wonders. These activities nurture analytical skills, critical thinking, and curiosity in physics, biology, chemistry, space, and technology.

Available on Amazon!

(Scan the QR code to visit Amazon store)

Prepare to embark on an exciting journey where the joy of **cooking** meets the wonder of **science**! This vibrant cookbook is packed with **25 delicious cooking experiments** crafted for young chefs, aged 7 to 12, offering diverse hands-on experiments across five captivating sections: Bake, Grill, Boil, Fry, and Desserts.

Interactive Learning Experience: With step-by-step instructions, ingredient lists, and required equipment for each cooking experiment, **'Future Chef'** transforms the kitchen into a vivid laboratory. Through vibrant illustrations, scientific principles come alive, ensuring that each recipe is an engaging exploration of culinary science.

Available on Amazon!

(Scan the QR code to visit Amazon store)

Prepare your child for an exciting mathematical journey with **"Future Mathematician."** This extraordinary book is specially crafted for young minds, ages 7 to 12, making mathematics not just accessible but enjoyable, empowering them with the skills they need to tackle real-world math challenges.

Unlocking Mathematical Magic: Mathematics is everywhere around us, but sometimes it can seem disconnected from our daily lives. **"Future Mathematician"** breaks down these barriers, revealing the enchanting world of math that surrounds us every day. This book bridges the gap between the classroom and reality, showing kids the profound importance of math in their lives.

Made in the USA
Las Vegas, NV
15 November 2024

11820170R00044